Copyright Disclaimer

Light Language: A New Era

© 2024 Paula Wratten. All rights reserved.

The prior written permission of the publisher is required to reproduce, distribute, or transmit any part of this book in any form or by any means, including photocopying, recording, or other electronic or mechanical methods, except in the case of brief quotations embodied in critical reviews and certain other noncommercial uses permitted by copyright law. For permission requests, write to the publisher at the address below:

Paula Wratten (paulawratten@aol.com)

This book is a work of nonfiction. The experiences, stories, and practices described herein are based on the author's research and personal experiences, as well as testimonials from individuals who have engaged with Light Language. The author and publisher make no representations or warranties with respect to the accuracy or completeness of the contents of this book and disclaim any implied warranties of merchantability or fitness for a particular purpose.

The practices and exercises outlined in this book do not intend to substitute professional medical advice or treatment. Always seek the advice of your physician or other qualified health providers with any questions you may have regarding a medical condition. Reliance on any information provided in this book is solely at your own risk.

By reading this book, you confirm and accept the disclaimer, which states that the author and publisher cannot be held responsible for any damages resulting from its use. By reading this book, you acknowledge and agree with this disclaimer.

First Edition: 2024

Cover Design by: Amazon UK

Printed in the United Kingdom

Light Language: An Exploration into Cosmic Communication

Table of Contents

Chapter 1: Introduction to Light Language

What is Light Language?

Light language is an ancient and enigmatic form of communication that transcends the limitations of spoken and written languages. Rooted in the vibrations and frequencies of sound, symbols, and movement, light language serves as a bridge to higher realms of consciousness and spiritual dimensions. Unlike traditional languages, which rely on structured grammar and vocabulary, light language flows intuitively from the heart and soul, carrying with it profound healing energies and spiritual insights. Many people often describe it as the language of the soul or the language of light, as it bypasses the analytical mind and speaks directly to the deeper layers of our being. Practitioners of light language believe that it can activate dormant parts of our DNA, elevate our consciousness, and align us with our highest purpose.

 Light language serves as a multidimensional tool that practitioners use for a range of purposes, including personal healing, spiritual growth, and facilitating communication with higher beings and realms.

Its transformative power lies in its ability to resonate with the energetic frequencies of the universe, offering a direct and pure connection to the divine.

Origins and Beliefs
The concept of Light Language finds its roots in various spiritual and metaphysical traditions. It is believed to be a form of ancient communication used by advanced civilisations, including Lemuria and Atlantis. Proponents of Light Language assert that it is a tool for spiritual awakening, healing, and connecting with higher dimensions.

Sovereign Being Of Light

To be a sovereign being of light means to recognise and embody one's inherent divine nature, autonomy, and alignment with the highest aspects of self and universal consciousness. Spiritual traditions and metaphysical beliefs deeply root this concept, emphasising personal empowerment, spiritual awakening, and the realisation of one's true essence as a being of light. Here are the key aspects of what it means to be a sovereign being of light:

Recognising Divine Nature

Sovereign beings of light understand their connection to the universe and the oneness of existence. They express love, compassion, wisdom, and peace in their daily lives, embodying their divine nature. They practise self-mastery, taking responsibility for their thoughts, emotions, and actions. They free themselves from external influences and societal conditioning, making choices that align with their highest good and inner truth.

Alignment with Higher Self

- Connection to Higher Guidance: They maintain a strong connection with their higher self, inner guidance, or spiritual guides. This connection helps them navigate life with clarity and purpose.

- Intuitive Living: Sovereign beings of light rely on their intuition and inner knowing to make decisions, trusting the wisdom from within.

- Spiritual Awakening and Growth

- Continuous Evolution: Their commitment lies in their spiritual growth and constant evolution. This involves regular practices, such as meditation, energy healing, and self-reflection.

Transcending Ego: They work on transcending the ego, recognising that the ego's fears and desires can limit their true potential and understanding of reality.

- Living in Alignment with Universal Laws

- Law of Attraction: They understand and utilise the law of attraction, knowing that their thoughts and emotions create their reality.

- Law of One: They live by the principle of the law of one, which states that all beings are one and that acts of service to others are acts of service to oneself.

- Radiating Light and Love

- Being a Lightworker: Sovereign beings of light often take on the role of lightworkers, spreading light, love, and positive energy wherever they go.

- Healing and Transformation: They contribute to the healing and transformation of the world by holding a high vibrational frequency and serving as examples of awakened consciousness.

- Maintaining Energetic Integrity

- Healthy Boundaries: They maintain healthy energetic boundaries, ensuring that they do not take on negative energies from others and preserve their energy field.

- Regular Cleansing: They practise regular energetic cleansing to keep their energy field clear and vibrant.

- Manifesting Reality

- Co-Creation with the Universe: They actively co-create their reality with the universe, setting clear intentions and taking inspired action towards their goals.

- Abundance Mindset: They cultivate an abundance mindset, understanding that the universe is infinitely abundant and that they are deserving of all the good it has to offer.

- Practices to Embody Sovereignty and Light

- Meditation and Mindfulness: Regular meditation and mindfulness practices help maintain a connection with the higher self and foster inner peace.

- Energy Healing: Practices like Reiki, chakra balancing, and aura cleansing support energetic integrity and healing.

- Affirmations and Mantras: Positive affirmations and mantras can reinforce one's divine nature and empower self-mastery.

- Journaling: Keeping a journal can aid in self-reflection and the process of spiritual growth.

- Service to Others: Acts of kindness and service to others amplify the light one radiates and reinforce the interconnectedness of all beings.

Being a sovereign being of light is a profound state of spiritual awareness and personal empowerment. It involves recognising one's divine nature, maintaining autonomy, aligning with the higher self, and living in accordance with universal principles of love, unity, and light. By embodying these qualities, individuals can lead fulfilling, purpose-driven lives and contribute positively to the collective consciousness.

Chapter 2: Historical Perspectives

Ancient Civilisations

The lost civilisations of Lemuria and Atlantis are often associated with Light Language. These societies are said to have had advanced knowledge of spirituality, energy work, and communication with higher realms. Light Language was an integral part of their daily lives, used for healing, meditation, and connecting with divine beings.

Indigenous Cultures

Indigenous cultures worldwide have their own versions of Light Language. For instance, Native American tribes use specific chants and symbols in their rituals that convey deep spiritual meanings. Similarly, Aboriginal Australians have a rich tradition of storytelling through song lines, which are believed to be a form of Light Language.

Mystical Traditions

Mystical traditions such as Kabbalah, Sufism, and Gnosticism also hint at the existence of a universal language. In these traditions, sacred sounds, symbols, and movements are used to connect with higher realms and access hidden knowledge.

Exploring the Mystical Realm of Lemurian Light Language

In the expansive domain of spiritual practices, Lemurian Light Language is an enigmatic and fascinating phenomenon that continues to captivate seekers of esoteric wisdom. Rooted in the ancient lore of Lemuria, a lost continent believed to have existed in the Pacific Ocean, this mystical language is thought to be a conduit for higher consciousness and interdimensional communication.

Light Language in Our Ancient Past

Ancient Civilisations and Light Language

Lemuria and Atlantis

Lemuria and Atlantis are often cited as advanced ancient civilisations with a deep understanding of spiritual and metaphysical concepts. According to legend, these societies used Light Language as a primary mode of communication. It wasn't just spoken words, but a complex mode of communication encompassing sounds, symbols, and gestures that connected with higher frequencies.

Lemuria:

- Lemurians had a harmonious bond with nature and communicated with plants, animals, and elemental beings through Light Language. This communication was said to involve a deep understanding of vibrational frequencies and the natural world's energy.

- Healing Practices: Light Language was integral to their healing practices. By using specific sounds and symbols, healers aligned and balanced individuals' energy fields, leading to improved physical, emotional, and spiritual health.

Atlantis:

- Technological Advancements: Atlanteans reportedly used Light Language in conjunction with advanced technologies, such as crystal technology, to harness and direct energy. This combination allowed them to achieve feats that seem miraculous by today's standards.

- Spiritual Teachings: Atlantean spiritual teachings emphasised the importance of Light Language for personal and collective evolution. It was used in rituals, meditation, and education, serving as a tool for accessing higher wisdom and divine knowledge.

Indigenous Cultures and Light Language

Native American Tribes

Many Native American tribes have traditions that involve using sounds, chants, and symbols believed to carry spiritual significance. These practices are reminiscent of Light Language and reflect a deep connection to the spiritual realms.

- Chanting and Singing: Native American ceremonies often include chanting and singing, which are thought to invoke spiritual energies and connect with ancestors. These vocalisations can be seen as a form of Light Language, conveying messages beyond the ordinary scope of words.

- Sacred Symbols: Tribal art and symbols, such as those used in sand paintings or beadwork, carry meanings that transcend their visual appearance. They are used to tell stories, pass down wisdom, and connect with the spiritual world.

Aboriginal Australians

Aboriginal Australians have a rich tradition of storytelling through song lines, which are believed to map the land and the spiritual paths of their ancestors.

- Songlines: These are paths across the land that are recorded in songs, stories, dance, and painting. They can be seen as a form of Light Language, encoding information about geography, history, and spiritual knowledge in a non-linear, vibrational form.

- Dreamtime: Aboriginal spirituality includes the concept of Dreamtime, a sacred era in which ancestral beings created the world. Communication during Dreamtime is thought to involve a form of Light Language, where songs and symbols connect the people to their origins and the land.

Mystical Traditions and Light Language

Kabbalah

In the mystical Jewish tradition of Kabbalah, there is a belief in the power of sacred sounds and letters.

- Hebrew Letters: Each Hebrew letter is considered a building block of creation, with its own unique energy and significance. By arranging these letters in sacred texts and chants, it is believed to have an effect on both the spiritual and physical realms, much like Light Language.

- Meditative Practices: Kabbalistic meditation often involves focusing on specific sounds, letters, and words to elevate consciousness and connect with the divine. These practices resonate with the idea of using vibrational frequencies for spiritual growth.

Sufism

Sufism, the mystical branch of Islam, emphasises the use of sound and music for spiritual development.

- Dhikr: The practice of Dhikr involves the repetitive chanting of divine names and phrases. This practice is aimed at achieving a state of spiritual ecstasy and closeness to God, akin to the use of Light Language for connecting with higher realms.

- Whirling Dervishes: The Sufi practice of whirling, accompanied by music and chanting, is designed to induce a trance state and facilitate communication with the divine. The movements and sounds used are deeply symbolic and resonate with the principles of Light Language.

Gnosticism

Gnosticism, an ancient belief system that emphasises personal spiritual knowledge (gnosis) over orthodox teachings, also has elements reminiscent of Light Language.

- Sacred Sounds and Symbols: Gnostic texts often refer to the use of sacred sounds and symbols to access hidden knowledge and connect with higher dimensions. These practices align with the idea of Light Language as a tool for spiritual enlightenment.

The concept of Light Language is deeply rooted in our ancient past, appearing in various forms across different cultures and mystical traditions. From the advanced civilisations of Lemuria and Atlantis to indigenous practices and mystical teachings, Light Language has been a tool for communication, healing, and spiritual growth throughout history. By understanding and connecting with these ancient traditions, we can tap into the timeless wisdom encoded in Light Language and enhance our own spiritual journeys.

The Origins of Lemurian Light Language

The legend of Lemuria, akin to the tales of Atlantis, speaks of an advanced civilisation that flourished thousands of years ago. Lemurians are often depicted as enlightened beings with profound spiritual knowledge and abilities. The concept of Lemurian Light Language emerges from this mythos, suggesting that the Lemurians used a unique form of communication that transcends the limitations of spoken and written words.

People consider Lemurian Light Language to be a sacred and vibrational form of expression. It is believed to encompass sounds, tones, and symbols that resonate at high frequencies, facilitating a direct connection to the divine and the cosmos. Practitioners often describe it as a language of the soul, capable of conveying complex emotions, intentions, and spiritual truths in a pure and unfiltered form.

The Structure and Expression of Light Language

Unlike conventional languages, Lemurian Light Language does not adhere to grammatical rules or syntax. Instead, it is an intuitive and spontaneous mode of expression. Those who channel this language may produce vocal sounds, sing, or create intricate hand gestures and symbols. Each expression is unique to the individual and the moment, shaped by their inner guidance and spiritual attunement.

The vocal aspect of Light Language often includes harmonic tones, melodies, and non-verbal utterances that seem otherworldly. These sounds are said to activate energy centers within the body, align chakras, and facilitate healing on physical, emotional, and spiritual levels. Some practitioners also incorporate written symbols, which they claim hold specific energetic signatures and can be used in meditative practices or as talismans.

The Purpose and Benefits of Lemurian Light Language

Proponents of Lemurian Light Language believe it serves several profound purposes:

1. Spiritual Awakening and Ascension: By attuning to the frequencies of Light Language, individuals may experience heightened states of consciousness and a deeper connection to their higher self and the divine. This can accelerate their spiritual growth and ascension process.

2. Healing and Transformation: The vibrational nature of Light Language is thought to penetrate deeply into the energy body, releasing blockages and promoting holistic healing. It can help in transmuting negative energies and patterns, leading to emotional and psychological transformation.

3. Interdimensional Communication: Some view Light Language as a tool for communicating with higher dimensional beings, such as angels, spirit guides, and extraterrestrial entities. It is seen as a universal language that transcends earthly limitations and fosters cosmic unity.

4. Creative Expression and Manifestation: Engaging with Light Language can unlock creative potentials and aid in manifesting

desires by aligning one's intentions with the universal flow of energy.

Learning and Experiencing Lemurian Light Language

Learning Lemurian Light Language is less about formal instruction and more about personal discovery and spiritual practice. We encourage those interested in exploring this mystical language to meditate, connect with their intuition, and allow the expressions to flow naturally. Workshops, guided sessions, and attunements led by experienced practitioners can also provide valuable support and insights.

Experiencing Lemurian Light Language can be deeply moving and transformative. Whether through listening to recordings, participating in group sessions, or channelling it personally, individuals often report feelings of profound peace, clarity, and a sense of coming home to their true selves.

Lemurian Light Language remains a mysterious and awe-inspiring aspect of spiritual exploration. Rooted in the mythos of an ancient and enlightened civilisation, it offers a unique pathway to higher consciousness, healing, and interdimensional communication. For those willing to open their hearts and minds to its frequencies, the Lemurian Light Language can be a powerful tool for personal and collective transformation, guiding humanity toward a more harmonious and enlightened future.

The Spiritual Role of the Pleiadians in Light Language and Earth's Development

Many spiritual traditions and metaphysical communities have considered the Pleiadians, a group of extraterrestrial beings from the Pleiades star cluster as highly evolved, benevolent beings who play a crucial role in the spiritual evolution of humanity. Many spiritual traditions and metaphysical communities have long considered star clusters as highly evolved, benevolent beings who play a crucial role in the spiritual evolution of humanity. Their influence is particularly noted in the realms of light language and Earth's developmental journey towards higher consciousness. This essay explores the spiritual role of the Pleiadians in these contexts, highlighting their contributions and the transformative impact they have on Earth's spiritual landscape.

The Pleiadians: Who Are They?

The Pleiadians are often depicted as highly advanced, multidimensional beings with a deep connection to the Source and divine energy. They are believed to have transcended the limitations of the third-dimensional existence, operating from higher dimensions that allow them to access profound spiritual wisdom and abilities. The Pleiadians are seen as guardians and guides, committed to assisting humanity in its evolutionary process.

Light Language and the Pleiadians

Light language is a form of communication that transcends traditional human language. It is a multidimensional expression of energy, often consisting of sounds, symbols, and movements that carry specific frequencies and codes designed to activate, heal, and transform.

1. Transmission of Light Codes: The Pleiadians are considered masters of light language, and they use it to transmit light codes—packets of information encoded with spiritual knowledge and energetic frequencies. These light codes can activate dormant DNA, enhance psychic abilities, and accelerate spiritual growth. Through channelling, meditation, and dreams, individuals can receive these light codes, which are then integrated into their energetic field to facilitate personal and collective evolution.

2. Healing and Activation: Pleiadian light language is renowned for its healing properties. The vibrations and frequencies embedded in light language can penetrate deep into the physical, emotional, and spiritual bodies, releasing blockages, healing traumas, and activating higher states of consciousness. Practitioners who channel Pleiadian light language often report profound healing experiences and a greater sense of alignment with their true selves.

3. Enhanced Communication with Higher Realms: By engaging with Pleiadian light language, individuals can enhance their ability to communicate with higher realms. This communication is not limited to words, but includes receiving intuitive insights, visions, and a deeper understanding of spiritual truths. Light language serves as a bridge, connecting humans with their higher selves, spirit guides, and other benevolent beings in the universe.

The Pleiadians and Earth's Development

The Pleiadians are believed to have a longstanding relationship with Earth and humanity. Their role in Earth's development is multifaceted, encompassing spiritual guidance, technological influence, and ecological stewardship.

1. Spiritual Guidance: The Pleiadians have been guiding humanity through various stages of spiritual awakening. They provide teachings on love, compassion, unity, and the interconnectedness of all life. These teachings help humanity move beyond the limitations of fear, separation, and materialism, paving the way for a more enlightened and harmonious existence.

2. Technological Influence: There are claims that the Pleiadians have influenced human technological advancements, particularly those that promote clean energy and sustainable living. They are believed to share knowledge that can help humanity develop technologies aligned with the natural laws of the universe, fostering a more sustainable and balanced relationship with the Earth.

3. Ecological Stewardship: The Pleiadians emphasise the importance of caring for the Earth. They teach that the planet is a living being that requires respect and protection. Through their guidance, many individuals and groups have found inspiration to engage in environmental conservation, permaculture, and other practices that support the health and vitality of the Earth.

4. Facilitating the Shift to Higher Consciousness: One of the most significant roles of the Pleiadians is facilitating humanity's shift to higher consciousness. They assist in the transition from the third-dimensional reality, characterised by duality and conflict, to higher dimensions of unity, peace, and unconditional love. This shift involves the activation of higher-dimensional awareness, the integration of the light body, and the alignment with the Earth's ascension process.

5. Assisting in Global Transformations: The Pleiadians are believed to be actively involved in assisting humanity during times of global transformation. They provide energetic support and guidance during significant planetary alignments, shifts in consciousness, and other pivotal moments in human history. People often feel their presence during meditation, global healing events, and other spiritual gatherings focused on collective upliftment.

The Pleiadians are believed to activate light language in humans through a series of spiritual and energetic processes. This activation can occur through various means, including direct contact, channelled transmissions, meditative practices, and personal spiritual development. Here is an exploration of how the Pleiadians might facilitate the activation of light language in humans:

Light Code Transmissions
Energetic Downloads: Pleiadians are known for transmitting energetic downloads that carry light codes—specific frequencies of light and information. These codes are designed to resonate with the recipient's energetic and cellular structure, activating dormant aspects of their DNA and higher consciousness.

Symbolic Representations: Light codes can also be received as visual symbols during meditation, dreams, or intuitive states. These symbols can then be drawn, visualised, or meditated upon to facilitate further activation of light language.

DNA Activation
Genetic Awakening: Pleiadian activations often involve the awakening of dormant DNA strands. Humans are believed to have multidimensional DNA that holds spiritual and cosmic information. Pleiadians can activate these dormant strands, allowing individuals to access higher states of consciousness and their innate ability to express light language.

Crystalline DNA Structure: The transformation of human DNA from a carbon-based to a crystalline-based structure is a concept in spiritual communities. Pleiadians are said to assist in this transformation, which enhances the ability to receive and transmit higher frequencies, including light language.

Healing and Clearing

Energetic Clearing: Before light language can be fully activated, individuals often need to undergo a process of energetic clearing and healing. This involves releasing old traumas, limiting beliefs, and energetic blockages that hinder the flow of higher frequencies.

Chakra Alignment: Pleiadians work on aligning and activating the chakras, particularly the throat chakra (for expression) and the heart chakra (for unconditional love). A balanced and open chakra system allows for the free flow of light language.

The activation of light language by the Pleiadians is a multifaceted process that involves direct energetic transmissions, meditative practices, DNA activations, and personal spiritual development. By engaging with these practices and remaining open to receiving higher frequencies, individuals can unlock their innate ability to express and work with light language.
This activation not only enhances personal spiritual growth but also contributes to the collective ascension of humanity and the Earth.

Summary

The Pleiadians play a profound spiritual role in the development of Earth and humanity through their teachings, guidance, and the transmission of light language. Their influence extends beyond mere communication, offering healing, activation, and the facilitation of humanity's spiritual evolution. By engaging with Pleiadian light language and embracing their teachings, individuals and communities can experience profound transformations, aligning more closely with higher states ofconsciousness and contributing to the collective ascension of the planet. The Pleiadians remind us of our interconnectedness, our divine nature, and our potential to create a harmonious and enlightened world.

The Central Sun And The Elementals

The concept of the central sun and the elementals holds a significant place in various spiritual and esoteric traditions, where it is believed to play a pivotal role in enhancing human consciousness and facilitating the download of light language. Many spiritual and esoteric traditions believe that light language holds a significant place and plays a pivotal role in enhancing human consciousness and facilitating the download of information from higher realms for spiritual growth and healing.

Symbolic and Spiritual Significance

Source of Divine Energy: The central sun is considered the origin of all light and energy in the universe. It is seen as the fountainhead of life force, spiritual illumination, and cosmic consciousness, providing the energetic sustenance for all existence.

Cosmic Centre: In many traditions, the central sun is imagined as a central point in the universe, such as the galactic centre. This central point is thought to be the anchor of the cosmic order, from which all creation emanates and to which all energy eventually returns.

Higher Consciousness: The central sun represents the highest consciousness and divine intelligence. It is associated with enlightenment, ultimate truth, and the purest form of spiritual wisdom. Connecting with the central sun is believed to raise one's vibrational frequency and align them with their higher self.

The Central Sun: A Source of Divine Illumination

The central sun, in spiritual metaphysics, is regarded as a cosmic source of divine light and energy. It is often associated with the galactic centre or an even higher central point in the universe, representing the ultimate source of spiritual light and wisdom. This central sun is not merely a physical entity, but a symbolic representation of the highest consciousness and divine intelligence.

Many people believe that the energy from the central sun permeates through various layers of existence, infusing them with light and raising their vibrational frequency. For individuals seeking to download light language, connecting with the central sun can be crucial. This connection facilitates a higher state of consciousness, enabling one to receive and integrate the high-frequency codes and messages embedded in light language.

By attuning to the central sun, individuals can align themselves with a higher source of wisdom and elevate their spiritual awareness, making the reception of light language more profound and effective.

The Elementals: Guardians of Nature's Wisdom

In esoteric traditions, people consider elementals as the spirits of nature that represent the fundamental forces of the natural world. They encompass a wide range of beings associated with the elements of earth, air, fire, and water. These entities are seen as the custodians of the natural order, maintaining balance and harmony within their respective domains.

The elementals play a crucial role in grounding and channelling the energies from the central sun into the earthly realm. As intermediaries between the physical and spiritual worlds, they help to stabilise and integrate the high-frequency energies that humans receive from higher dimensions. This grounding process is essential for the effective download of light language, ensuring that the received information can be assimilated and utilised in practical, everyday life.

Working with the elementals can enhance one's ability to download and interpret light language by fostering a deeper connection between nature and the fundamental elements of existence. Through rituals, meditations, and interactions with nature, individuals can invoke the assistance of the elementals to create a balanced and receptive state, conducive to receiving and integrating the light language.

Synergy of the Central Sun and the Elementals

The interaction between the central sun and the elementals creates a harmonious pathway for the download of light language. The central sun provides the high-frequency light and wisdom, while the elementals ensure that this energy is grounded and balanced within the human experience. This synergy is essential for the smooth transmission and integration of light language, allowing individuals to access higher states of consciousness and spiritual insight.

In summary, the central sun and the elementals play complementary roles in the process of downloading light language. The central sun offers the divine illumination necessary for higher spiritual communication, while the elementals ground this energy into the physical realm, ensuring its practical application and integration. By understanding and working with these spiritual forces, individuals can enhance their ability to receive and interpret light language, fostering greater spiritual growth and enlightenment.

Visualisation Technique: Elemental Dance to Connect with Elementals and Receive Light Language

This visualisation technique involves a meditative movement practice, which I will call the "Elemental Dance." It combines visualisation, intention, and physical movement to help you connect with the elementals and receive light language.

Preparation

Find a Quiet Space: Choose a quiet, comfortable place where you won't be disturbed. This could be indoors or in a natural setting, such as a garden or park.

Set Your Intention: Before you begin, set a clear intention to connect with the elementals and receive light language. You can say something like, "I intend to connect with the elementals and open myself to receiving the wisdom and activation of light language."

Ground Yourself: Take a few moments to ground yourself. Stand or sit with your feet flat on the ground, and take several deep breaths, feeling the connection between your body and the Earth.

The Elemental Dance

Begin with the Earth Element

> Visualisation: Close your eyes and visualise yourself standing in a lush forest. Imagine the roots of the trees connecting deeply with the Earth. Feel the stability and strength of the Earth beneath you.

> Movement: Start with slow, deliberate movements that mimic the grounding and stability of the Earth. You might imagine yourself as a tree, swaying gently in the wind but firmly rooted.

> Affirmation: Silently or aloud, repeat, "I am connected to the Earth. I am grounded and stable."

Move to the Water Element

Visualisation: Visualise a flowing river or a serene lake. Feel the fluidity and cleansing power of water.

Movement: Transition into flowing, wavelike movements. Imagine your body as water, moving gracefully and effortlessly.

Affirmation: Silently or aloud, repeat, "I am connected to the Water. I flow with ease and grace."

Transition to the Fire Element

Visualisation: Visualise a warm, glowing fire. Feel the energy, transformation, and passion of the fire.

Movement: Allow your movements to become more dynamic and expressive, embodying the energy and intensity of fire. You might incorporate quick, energetic gestures.

Affirmation: Silently or aloud, repeat, "I am connected to the Fire. I am passionate and transformative."

Engage with the Air Element

Visualisation: Visualise a clear, open sky with a gentle breeze. Feel the freedom and expansiveness of the air.

Movement: Let your movements become light and airy, like you're being lifted by the wind. You might incorporate spinning or reaching movements.

Affirmation: Silently or aloud, repeat, "I am connected to the Air. I am free and expansive."

Integrate All Elements

Visualisation: Visualise yourself standing at the centre of a circle, with each element represented around you. Feel the balanced presence of Earth, Water, Fire, and Air.

Movement: Allow your body to move intuitively, incorporating the qualities of all four elements. Trust that your movements are guided by the elementals.

Affirmation: Silently or aloud, repeat, "I am connected to all elements. I am balanced and whole."

Receiving Light Language

Open to Receive

Visualisation: Visualise a beam of light coming down from the central sun, entering through the crown of your head and filling your entire being with light.

Movement: Continue to move gently, allowing the light to flow through you. Trust that you are receiving the frequencies and codes of light language.

Affirmation: Silently or aloud, repeat, "I am open to receiving light language. I am aligned with divine wisdom."

Integration and Reflection

Stillness: Gradually bring your movements to a still point. Stand or sit quietly, feeling the energies and insights you've received.

Reflection: Take a few moments to reflect on any sensations, thoughts, or images that came to you during the practice. You might want to journal your experiences.

By engaging in the Elemental Dance, you create a dynamic and embodied connection with the elementals, which can facilitate the reception and integration of light language. You can adapt and personalise this practice to suit your own preferences and intuition.

Elves and gnomes, along with other elementals, are important in light language within spiritual and esoteric traditions. They are considered guardians and caretakers of nature. Each of them has distinct qualities and responsibilities that help with the transmission and grounding of light language. Let's take a closer look at what they do.

Elves

Nature Spirits and Guardians

1. Connection to Nature: Elves are often depicted as highly connected to the natural world, particularly forests, plants, and trees. They are considered guardians of nature, helping to maintain balance and harmony within their realms.

2. High Vibrational Beings: Elves are believed to exist at a high vibrational frequency, making them sensitive to subtle energies and capable of interacting with higher dimensions. This sensitivity allows them to act as intermediaries for light language, which is also a high-frequency form of communication.

Role in Light Language

1. Transmission and Interpretation: Elves can assist in the transmission and interpretation of light language. Their connection to higher realms allows them to understand and relay the subtle frequencies and codes of light language, helping humans to decode and integrate these energies.

2. Enhancing Intuition: By working with elves, individuals can enhance their intuitive abilities and deepen their connection to the natural world. This enhanced intuition can make it easier to receive and understand the messages conveyed through light language.

3. Healing and Harmonising: Elves can facilitate healing and harmonising energies, making the integration of light language smoother and more balanced. Their nurturing presence can help individuals release blockages and align with the frequencies of light language.

Gnomes

Earth Elementals and Stewards

1. Connection to the Earth: Gnomes are closely associated with the earth element, representing the solidity, stability, and nurturing aspects of the Earth. They are seen as protectors of the soil, minerals, and subterranean realms.

2. Grounding Energy: Gnomes are masters of grounding energy, making them essential for integrating spiritual experiences and high-frequency energies into the physical realm.

Role in Light Language

1. Grounding Light Codes: Gnomes play a crucial role in grounding the high-frequency light codes received through light language. They ensure that these energies are anchored into the Earth, allowing individuals to integrate and apply the wisdom in practical, everyday life.

2. Stabilising Energies: By working with gnomes, individuals can stabilise the intense energies of light language. This stabilisation helps to prevent overwhelm and ensures that the energies are assimilated in a balanced and sustainable way.

3. Facilitating Manifestation: Gnomes can assist in translating the spiritual insights and activations from light language into tangible outcomes. Their connection to the earth element helps individuals to manifest their intentions and spiritual growth into physical reality.

Practical Ways to Connect with Elves and Gnomes

1. Nature Immersion: Spending time in natural environments, such as forests or gardens, can help individuals connect with the energies of elves and gnomes. Observing and appreciating the beauty of nature can open channels of communication with these elementals.

2. Meditation and Visualisation: Meditative practices that focus on connecting with nature spirits can enhance one's ability to interact with elves and gnomes. Visualising encounters with these beings and inviting their presence can facilitate a deeper connection.

3. Rituals and Offerings: Performing rituals and making offerings, such as planting trees or creating sacred spaces in nature, can honour the presence of elves and gnomes. These actions demonstrate respect and invite their guidance and support.

4. Crystals and Earth Materials: Working with crystals and other earth materials can help attune individuals to the energies of gnomes. Using these materials in meditation or placing them in one's environment can enhance the grounding of light language energies.

Integration of Light Language with Elves and Gnomes

1. Balanced Approach: Elves and gnomes help ensure a balanced approach to integrating light language. While elves assist with the higher vibrational aspects and intuitive understanding, gnomes provide the grounding and practical application of these energies.

2. Holistic Transformation: By engaging with both elves and gnomes, individuals can achieve a holistic transformation, encompassing spiritual insight and physical manifestation. This balanced integration supports sustained spiritual growth and enhanced well-being.

In conclusion, elves and gnomes play essential roles in the reception, interpretation, and grounding of light language. Their unique qualities and connections to the natural and spiritual realms make them invaluable allies in the journey of spiritual evolution and the practical integration of divine energies.

Using A Mandala Of Light

A "mandala of light" is a spiritual and meditative tool that combines the traditional concept of a mandala with the symbolic and energetic qualities of light. Mandalas are intricate geometric patterns that represent the universe in Hindu and Buddhist symbolism, often used as a meditation aid to promote mindfulness and spiritual enlightenment. When combined with the concept of light, a mandala of light serves as a powerful visual and energetic focal point for spiritual practices.

Characteristics of a Mandala of Light

Geometric Symmetry: Like traditional mandalas, a mandala of light typically features a symmetrical design with intricate patterns radiating from a central point. This symmetry helps to focus the mind and create a sense of balance and harmony.

Radiance and Illumination: The mandala is often envisioned as being composed of or emanating light. This can include visualising the mandala glowing with vibrant colours, or seeing beams of light extending from the central point outward.

Symbolism: Each element within the mandala of light can hold specific symbolic meanings, representing various aspects of the cosmos, spiritual principles, or personal insights. The light aspect can symbolise divine wisdom, spiritual enlightenment, and the presence of higher consciousness.

Functions and Uses

Meditation and Focus: Meditating on a mandala of light can help deepen one's meditative state, enhance concentration, and promote inner peace. The visual and energetic aspects of the light help to uplift and purify the mind and spirit.

Spiritual Activation: A mandala of light can serve as a tool for spiritual activation, helping to align the individual with higher frequencies and divine energies. It can facilitate the reception of spiritual insights and the awakening of latent potentials within the individual.

Healing and Transformation: The light energy within the mandala can be used for healing and transformation, aiding in the release of negative energies, emotional blockages, and physical ailments. The visualised light can be directed to specific areas of the body or energy field to promote healing.

Manifestation: By focusing on a mandala of light, individuals can set intentions and visualise their desires manifesting in their lives. The mandala serves as a focal point to concentrate their energy and align it with their goals.

Creating and Using a Mandala of Light

Visualisation: Close your eyes and visualise a mandala composed of radiant light. See the intricate patterns glowing with vibrant colours, and feel the energy emanating from the central point.

Drawing or Painting: Create your mandala of light on paper or canvas using bright, luminous colours. As you draw or paint, infuse the mandala with your intentions and positive energy.

Digital Tools: Use digital tools to design a mandala of light. There are many apps and software programs available that allow you to create and customise mandalas with a variety of colours and patterns.

Guided Meditation: Listen to a guided meditation that focuses on visualising and working with a mandala of light. This can provide structure and guidance, especially for beginners.

Interactive Practice: Place a physical or digital representation of the mandala of light in your meditation space. Spend time each day focusing on it, allowing its energy to permeate your being and enhance your spiritual practice.

Integration with Elementals and Light Language

Elemental Connection: Incorporate the energies of the elementals into your mandala of light. Visualise the presence of earth, air, fire, and water within the mandala, and invite the elementals to assist in grounding and balancing the light energies.

Receiving Light Language: Use the mandala of light as a gateway for receiving light language. As you focus on the mandala, open yourself to the transmission of high-frequency codes and messages. Allow these energies to flow through you, activating and expanding your consciousness.

Balancing Energies: Work with the mandala of light to balance and harmonise the energies received from the elementals and light language. The mandala can serve as a stabilising force, integrating these diverse energies into a cohesive and aligned whole.

In summary, a mandala of light is a powerful spiritual tool that combines the geometric and symbolic aspects of traditional mandalas with the illuminating and transformative qualities of light. It can be used for meditation, spiritual activation, healing, and manifestation, and can be integrated with the energies of the elementals and light language for a holistic and profound spiritual practice.

Chapter 3: The Science Behind Light Language

Vibrations and Frequencies

At its core, Light Language operates on the principles of vibrations and frequencies. Every sound, symbol, and gesture in Light Language carries a specific vibrational frequency that resonates with different aspects of our being. This resonance can facilitate healing, spiritual awakening, and transformation.

Quantum Physics

Quantum physics provides a scientific framework for understanding Light Language. According to quantum theory, everything in the universe is interconnected through a web of energy. Light Language taps into this energy field, allowing for communication across different dimensions and levels of consciousness.

Neuroplasticity

The practice of Light Language can also be explained through the concept of neuroplasticity. Engaging with Light Language activates different parts of the brain, creating new neural pathways and enhancing cognitive flexibility. This can lead to increased intuition, creativity, and spiritual awareness.

Ancient Knowledge of Light Language within Our DNA

The Concept of Genetic Memory

The idea that our DNA holds ancient knowledge, including the understanding and ability to use Light Language, is rooted in the concept of genetic memory. Genetic memory suggests that certain experiences and knowledge can be passed down through generations at a cellular level. This concept aligns with the belief that Light Language is an intrinsic part of our being, waiting to be awakened.

Epigenetics and Spiritual Inheritance

Epigenetics, the study of how behaviours and environment can cause changes that affect the way our genes work, provides a scientific framework for understanding how spiritual knowledge, such as Light Language, might be inherited. Epigenetic changes can influence gene expression without altering the DNA sequence itself. These changes can be triggered by various factors, including spiritual practices, meditation, and exposure to high vibrational frequencies.

The Role of Junk DNA

A significant portion of our DNA, often referred to as "junk DNA," does not code for proteins and its function has long been a mystery. Some scientists and spiritual researchers speculate that this non-coding DNA may hold the key to our spiritual and cosmic heritage, including the knowledge of Light Language. It is believed that as we evolve and our consciousness expands, we may activate these dormant parts of our DNA, unlocking ancient knowledge and abilities.

New Theories on Junk DNA and Hidden Knowledge

For decades, scientists labelled a significant portion of the human genome as "junk DNA," believing it to be non-functional remnants of evolutionary history. However, emerging research and new theories suggest that this so-called junk DNA may hold crucial hidden knowledge and play vital roles in various biological processes and even consciousness itself. This shift in understanding challenges long-held assumptions and opens up fascinating possibilities for the fields of genetics, medicine, and spirituality.

Traditionally, junk DNA referred to the 98% of the human genome that does not code for proteins. Initially, the scientific community believed that only the 2% of DNA that directly codes for proteins was functional, while regarding the rest as evolutionary debris.

However, as genetic research has advanced, scientists have uncovered the potential functions of these vast stretches of DNA. One of the most compelling theories is that junk DNA is involved in regulating gene expression. Scientists have begun to uncover the potential functions of these vast stretches of DNA, which may contain regulatory elements that influence when, where, and how genes are turned on and off, thereby playing a crucial role in cellular function and development.

Another intriguing theory proposes that junk DNA acts as a repository for hidden knowledge and complex biological information. Researchers have discovered that non-coding DNA sequences are conserved across different species, suggesting that they are subject to selective pressures and have important functions. These sequences may encode information that is critical for the organism's adaptation and survival, functioning in ways that are not yet understood by science. This hidden knowledge could include instructions for complex biological processes, developmental pathways, and responses to environmental stimuli.

Besides its biological roles, some theories suggest that junk DNA may be linked to consciousness and higher cognitive functions. Proponents of this idea argue that the vast non-coding regions of the genome might serve as a biological interface for accessing and processing information beyond the physical realm. This concept aligns with the notion of DNA as a quantum system, where genetic material is not only a biochemical entity, but also a conduit for energy and information. According to this view, junk DNA could be involved in phenomena such as intuition, psychic abilities, and other aspects of human consciousness that transcend our current scientific understanding.

Epigenetics, the study of changes in gene expression caused by mechanisms other than changes in the DNA sequence, also sheds light on the potential importance of junk DNA. Epigenetic modifications, such as DNA methylation and histone modification, often occur in non-coding regions and play a key role in regulating gene activity. Environmental factors, lifestyle, and even emotional states can influence these modifications, suggesting that junk DNA dynamically participates in how our genes respond to external and internal conditions. This dynamic interaction highlights the potential for junk DNA to store and transmit information about an individual's experiences, contributing to the complexity and adaptability of the human genome.

Recent technological advancements, such as CRISPR-Cas9 gene editing and advanced genomic sequencing, have enabled scientists to explore junk DNA more thoroughly. These tools allow for precise manipulation and observation of non-coding regions, revealing their potential functions and interactions with the rest of the genome. Through these studies, researchers are beginning to uncover the intricate regulatory networks embedded within junk DNA, providing insights into how these sequences contribute to health, disease, and overall genetic diversity.

The implications of these new theories are profound. If junk DNA is indeed functional and contains hidden knowledge, it could revolutionize our understanding of genetics, evolution, and human potential. In medicine, this knowledge could lead to breakthroughs in diagnosing and treating complex diseases that are influenced by non-coding DNA. It could also pave the way for personalized medicine approaches that consider the unique regulatory landscapes of individuals' genomes.

Moreover, the idea that junk DNA might be connected to consciousness and higher cognitive functions invites a paradigm shift in how we view human potential and the nature of reality. It suggests that our genetic makeup is not just a blueprint for our physical bodies but also a gateway to deeper dimensions of existence. This perspective encourages a holistic approach to health and well-being, integrating physical, mental, and spiritual dimensions.

The new theories on junk DNA and hidden knowledge challenge the outdated notion of non-coding DNA as useless genetic material. Instead, they reveal the potential for these regions to play critical roles in gene regulation, adaptation, and possibly even consciousness. As research continues to unveil the mysteries of junk DNA, we may find ourselves on the brink of a genetic revolution that transforms our understanding of life, health, and human potential.

DNA Activation Techniques

Many practitioners of Light Language believe in the possibility of DNA activation through various techniques. These techniques are designed to awaken our latent spiritual potential and reconnect us with our ancient knowledge.

Meditation and Visualisation

Meditation and visualisation are powerful tools for activating DNA. By entering a deep meditative state and visualising light and energy flowing through your DNA, you can stimulate the awakening of dormant knowledge. Specific guided meditations for DNA activation often focus on light codes, sacred geometry, and the intention to awaken your inner wisdom.

Sound and Frequency Healing

Sound and frequency healing involve using specific tones, chants, and vibrations to influence the body at a cellular level. Since Light Language is inherently connected to vibrational frequencies, these practices can help activate DNA and facilitate the flow of ancient knowledge. Listening to or creating sounds in Light Language can resonate with your DNA, promoting healing and awakening.

Energy Work and Healing Modalities

Various energy healing modalities, such as Reiki, crystal healing, and quantum touch, can also support DNA activation. These practices work by channelling high-frequency energy into the body, which can stimulate the awakening of dormant DNA and enhance your connection to Light Language.

Case Studies and Experiences

Personal Accounts of DNA Activation

Many individuals who practise Light Language report profound experiences of DNA activation. For example, during deep meditative states or energy healing sessions, they often describe sensations of energy moving through their bodies, spontaneous understanding of Light Language symbols, and a heightened sense of spiritual awareness.

- Anna's Experience: Anna, a Light Language practitioner, describes a meditation session where she felt a surge of energy in her spine, followed by a vision of ancient symbols. Over time, she realised these symbols were part of Light Language and began incorporating them into her healing practice.

- David's Journey: David experienced a spontaneous activation of his DNA during a sound healing session. As the practitioner chanted in Light Language, David felt his body vibrating and saw flashes of light. He later found himself intuitively speaking Light Language, which he uses for personal healing and spiritual growth.

The Spiritual Significance

The activation of ancient knowledge within our DNA is seen as a crucial step in our spiritual evolution. It reconnects us with our cosmic heritage, enhances our intuitive abilities, and deepens our understanding of the universe. By embracing Light Language and exploring its connection to our DNA, we can access a wealth of wisdom and healing potential that has been dormant within us for centuries.

Integrating Ancient Knowledge into Modern Life

As we awaken to the ancient knowledge within our DNA, it is essential to integrate this wisdom into our daily lives. Regular practice of Light Language, mindfulness, and staying connected to our spiritual communities allows us to achieve this integration. By doing so, we honour our ancestral heritage and contribute to the collective awakening of humanity.

The ancient knowledge of Light Language within our DNA is a testament to our profound connection with the cosmos and our spiritual heritage. As we explore and activate this knowledge, we open ourselves to a deeper understanding of who we are and our purpose in the universe. Through meditation, sound healing, and other spiritual practices, we can awaken our dormant potential and embrace the transformative power of Light Language.

Neuroplasticity and the Practice of Light Language

Understanding Neuroplasticity

Neuroplasticity is the brain's ability to reorganise itself by forming new neural connections throughout life. This remarkable capacity allows the brain to adapt to new experiences, learn new information, and recover from injuries. Engaging in new activities, learning new skills, and practicing different forms of communication can significantly influence neuroplasticity.

Light Language and Brain Activation

The practice of Light Language involves unique sounds, symbols, and movements that engage the brain in novel ways. This engagement can stimulate neuroplasticity, fostering new neural pathways and enhancing cognitive flexibility. Here's how Light Language can influence the brain:

Auditory Processing

When you listen to or produce sounds in Light Language, you activate various regions of the brain involved in auditory processing. These areas include the primary auditory cortex, which processes basic sound information, and the superior temporal gyrus, which helps interpret complex sounds like speech. The unusual and non-linear nature of Light Language sounds can challenge and stimulate these auditory regions, promoting neural growth and adaptation.

Motor Coordination

Incorporating movements and gestures into Light Language practice engages the motor cortex, responsible for planning, controlling, and executing voluntary movements. Coordinating hand gestures, body movements, or dance with vocalisations in Light Language requires precise motor skills and can lead to the formation of new motor pathways in the brain.

Visual Imagery

Using symbols and visual representations in Light Language activates the visual cortex. Creating or interpreting these symbols can stimulate visual processing areas, enhancing your ability to visualise and comprehend abstract forms. This engagement can improve visual-spatial skills and promote creativity.

Emotional and Limbic System Activation

Light Language often evokes deep emotional responses, activating the limbic system, which is responsible for emotions, memory, and arousal. The emotional resonance of Light Language can help process and release stored emotions, contributing to emotional healing and balance. This activation can lead to more profound emotional awareness and resilience.

Enhancing Cognitive Flexibility

Cognitive flexibility is the mental ability to switch between thinking about different concepts and to think about multiple concepts simultaneously. Practicing Light Language can enhance cognitive flexibility by encouraging the brain to process information in non-traditional ways. The brain must adapt to understanding and producing unconventional sounds, symbols, and movements, leading to increased mental agility and problem-solving skills.

Benefits of Neuroplasticity through Light Language

Improved Intuition and Creativity

Engaging with Light Language can enhance your intuition and creativity. The novel and abstract nature of Light Language encourages the brain to think outside conventional patterns, fostering innovative thinking and intuitive insights. Many practitioners report heightened creativity in their artistic endeavours and an increased ability to access intuitive guidance.

Emotional Healing and Well-being

The practice of Light Language can promote emotional healing by facilitating the release of stored emotions and trauma. Engaging with the emotional aspects of Light Language can help you process and integrate these experiences, leading to greater emotional balance and well-being. A sense of inner peace and clarity often accompanies this emotional release.

Enhanced Learning and Memory

Neuroplasticity enhances the brain's capacity to learn and remember new information. Practicing Light Language can stimulate the brain's learning centres, improving memory retention and recall. This cognitive enhancement can benefit various aspects of life, from academic pursuits to daily problem-solving.

Practical Exercises to Promote Neuroplasticity with Light Language

Daily Light Language Practice

Incorporate Light Language into your daily routine. Spend a few minutes each day speaking, chanting, or singing in Light Language. Allow yourself to be spontaneous and free, focusing on the sounds and how they resonate within you. This regular practice will stimulate auditory processing and enhance neural pathways related to sound and speech.

Creative Symbolism

Create and interpret symbols in Light Language. Draw or paint symbols that come to you intuitively, or try automatic writing. Spend time meditating on these symbols, allowing your mind to explore their meanings. This visual engagement can stimulate the visual cortex and enhance creativity.

Movement and Dance

Incorporate movement and dance into your Light Language practice. Allow your body to move freely in response to the sounds you create or hear. This physical expression engages the motor cortex and promotes coordination and fluidity in your movements, stimulating neuroplasticity.

Emotional Expression

Use Light Language to express your emotions. When you feel strong emotions, whether joy, sadness, anger, or love, vocalise them in Light Language. Allow the sounds to carry the emotional energy, facilitating emotional release and healing. This practice engages the limbic system and promotes emotional well-being.

Case Studies and Experiences

Sarah's Journey to Emotional Healing

Sarah, a Light Language practitioner, used vocalisations and symbols to express her deep-seated emotions. Over time, she noticed a significant reduction in anxiety and a greater sense of inner peace. Her brain scans showed increased activity in the limbic system, correlating with her improved emotional state.

Michael's Creative Breakthrough

Michael, an artist, began incorporating Light Language into his creative process. He found that his artwork became more vibrant and expressive, and he experienced frequent bursts of inspiration. Neuroimaging revealed enhanced connectivity between the visual and auditory cortices, supporting his heightened creativity.

The practice of Light Language offers a unique and powerful way to stimulate neuroplasticity, enhancing various aspects of brain function and overall well-being. By engaging in this ancient form of cosmic communication, you can unlock new levels of intuition, creativity, and emotional balance. Embrace the practice of Light Language as a journey of personal and spiritual growth, and experience the transformative power of neuroplasticity in your life.

Chapter 4: Learning and Practicing Light Language

Awakening Your Inner Light Language

Everyone has the potential to understand and use Light Language. The first step is to quiet the mind and connect with your inner self. Meditation, breathwork, and other mindfulness practices can help you tune into the subtle frequencies of Light Language.

Techniques and Exercises

- Sound Activation: Start by making spontaneous sounds and allowing your voice to flow naturally. Don't worry about meaning or structure; focus on the vibrations and how they make you feel.

- Symbolic Writing: Allow your hand to move freely on paper, creating symbols and shapes. This automatic writing can help you access deeper levels of consciousness.

- Movement and Gesture: Incorporate movement into your practice. Allow your body to express itself through dance or gestures that feel natural and intuitive.

Hand symbols, also known as hand gestures or mudras, are an integral aspect of Light Language. They involve specific hand positions and movements that convey energetic and spiritual messages, facilitate healing, and connect with higher dimensions. These gestures, often guided intuitively, can be used independently or in combination with vocalisations and visualisations. Here's an in-depth look at the role and significance of hand symbols in Light Language.

The Role of Hand Symbols

1. Energy Activation and Direction: Many people believe that hand symbols activate and direct energy within the body and the surrounding environment. Different gestures can open energy pathways, clear blockages, and focus on healing intentions.

2. Spiritual Communication: Hand symbols serve as a form of non-verbal communication with higher realms, including spiritual guides, angels, and other benevolent entities. These gestures can convey messages, invoke protection, and request guidance.

3. Enhancing Meditation and Healing: Incorporating hand symbols into meditation and healing practices can deepen the experience, amplify the effects, and facilitate a stronger connection with the divine.

Common Hand Symbols and Their Meanings

While individuals often have unique hand symbols in Light Language based on their intuitive guidance, they can also adapt common gestures from various spiritual traditions into Light Language practices.

1. **Gyan Mudra (Mudra of Knowledge):**

   How to Perform: Touch the tip of the thumb to the tip of the index finger, with the other three fingers extended.

   Meaning and Use: Enhances concentration and wisdom, promotes mental clarity, and stimulates the root chakra.

Anjali Mudra (Prayer Gesture):

   How to Perform: Press the palms together at the heart centre with fingers pointing upward.

   Meaning and Use: Signifies greeting, gratitude, and deep respect; balances the right and left sides of the body and mind.

Shuni Mudra (Mudra of Patience):

   How to Perform: Touch the tip of the thumb to the tip of the middle finger, with the other fingers extended.

   Meaning and Use: Encourages patience and discipline, helps in grounding and centreing energy.

Prana Mudra (Mudra of Life):

How to Perform: Touch the tips of the thumb, ring finger, and little finger together, keeping the other two fingers straight.

Meaning and Use: Increases vitality and energy, strengthens the immune system, and activates the root chakra.

Apana Mudra (Mudra of Digestion):

How to Perform: Touch the tips of the thumb, middle finger, and ring finger together, keeping the other two fingers straight.

Meaning and Use: Aids in detoxification and digestion, releases negative energy, and promotes inner purification.

Integrating Hand Symbols in Light Language Practice

1. Intuitive Gestures: Trust your intuition to guide the creation of hand symbols. During meditation or healing sessions, allow your hands to move freely and naturally, forming gestures that feel energetically significant.

2. Intentional Movements: Combine hand symbols with vocalisations, visualisations, and breathwork. Set a clear intention for each gesture to direct its energy and purpose.

3. Energy Sensing: Pay attention to the sensations in your hands and body as you perform different hand symbols. Notice any shifts in energy, emotions, or physical sensations, which can provide insights into the effectiveness of the gestures.

4. Sacred Space: Create a dedicated space for your Light Language practice. Enhance the atmosphere with elements such as crystals, candles, and sacred objects to support the energetic flow and intention of your hand symbols.

Hand symbols in Light Language are a powerful tool for directing energy, enhancing spiritual communication, and deepening meditation and healing practices. By exploring both traditional and intuitive hand gestures, practitioners can access a richer, more nuanced experience of Light Language. These gestures serve as a bridge between the physical and spiritual realms, facilitating profound connections and transformations.

Sounds To Activate Light Language

Creating an alphabet for light language transmission involves assigning symbols or sounds to represent different aspects of energy, intention, or meaning. Since light language is highly intuitive and personal, the symbols or sounds you choose can be unique to your own practice. Here's a basic example of an alphabet for light language transmission:

A - Ah

- Represents openness, receptivity, and acceptance.

B - Bah

- Symbolises grounding, stability, and connection to the earth.

C - Chay

- Signifies clarity, insight, and inner vision.

D - Dah

- Represents divine guidance, protection, and wisdom.

E - Eh

- Symbolises expansion, growth, and evolution.

F - Fah

- Signifies flow, movement, and flexibility.

G - Guh

- Represents gratitude, appreciation, and abundance.

H - Hah

- Symbolises healing, harmony, and wholeness.

I - Ee

- Signifies intention, focus, and manifestation.

J - Juh

- Represents joy, celebration, and creativity.

K - Kah

- Symbolises strength, resilience, and empowerment.

L - Lah

- Signifies love, compassion, and kindness.

M - Mah

- Represents manifestation, materialisation, and creation.

N - Nah

- Symbolises nurturing, support, and nourishment.

O - Oh

- Signifies oneness, unity, and interconnectedness.

P - Pah

- Represents protection, shielding, and safety.

Q - Quah

- Symbolises quiet, stillness, and inner peace.

R - Rah

- Signifies release, letting go, and surrender.

S - Sss

- Represents serenity, tranquillity, and balance.

T - Tah

- Symbolises transformation, renewal, and rebirth.

U - Oo

- Signifies unity, harmony, and cooperation.

V - Vah

- Represents vitality, energy, and life force.

W - Wah

- Symbolises wisdom, intuition, and spiritual insight.

X - Ex

- Signifies exploration, adventure, and discovery.

Y - Yah

- Represents youthfulness, freshness, and renewal.

Z - Zzz

- Symbolises relaxation, rest, and rejuvenation.

Remember, this is just a basic example, and you can create your own alphabet for light language transmission based on your intuition, personal experiences, and the meanings you attribute to each symbol or sound. Allow your creativity to flow and trust in the messages that come through as you engage with your light language practice.

Chapter 5: Applications and Benefits

Applications and Benefits of Light Language

Light language is a profound and multifaceted tool in the realm of spiritual and energetic practices. It encompasses an array of sounds, symbols, movements, and frequencies that transcend conventional linguistic boundaries, offering a direct line of communication with the soul and higher realms of consciousness. As more individuals explore its depths, the applications and benefits of light language become increasingly apparent, illuminating its potential to transform, heal, and elevate human experience.

One of the primary applications of light language is in personal healing. Practitioners channel light language to clear energetic blockages, release emotional traumas, and restore balance to the physical, emotional, and spiritual bodies. The high-frequency vibrations of light language can penetrate deeply into the cellular and energetic structures, promoting profound healing and rejuvenation. This process not only alleviates physical ailments but also addresses underlying emotional and psychological issues, facilitating holistic well-being. By engaging with light language, individuals can experience a sense of renewal and harmony that conventional methods might not achieve.

Light language is also a powerful tool for spiritual growth and awakening. It serves as a catalyst for expanding consciousness, activating dormant aspects of the DNA, and aligning individuals with their higher self and soul purpose. Through the practice of light language, one can access higher states of awareness and connect with the divine, gaining insights and guidance that are crucial for spiritual evolution. This connection fosters a deeper understanding of one's true nature and place in the cosmos, leading to a more purposeful and enlightened life.

The transformative power of light language lies in its ability to dissolve the barriers between the physical and spiritual realms, allowing for a seamless flow of divine energy and wisdom.

Another significant application of light language is in the realm of energetic protection and cleansing. The vibrations and frequencies emitted through light language can create a protective shield around individuals, safeguarding them from negative energies and influences. This protective barrier is particularly beneficial for empaths and susceptible individuals who are prone to absorbing external energies. Additionally, light language can be used to cleanse and purify spaces, objects, and environments, removing stagnant or harmful energies and creating a more harmonious and supportive atmosphere.

In the context of communication with higher beings and realms, light language acts as a universal medium that transcends the limitations of human language. It facilitates direct communication with angels, spirit guides, extraterrestrial beings, and other multidimensional entities. This ability to communicate across different planes of existence provides access to a wealth of knowledge, wisdom, and support that can aid in one's spiritual journey. The messages and energies received through light language are often imbued with divine love and guidance, offering clarity and direction in times of uncertainty.

The benefits of light language extend to creative expression and artistic endeavours as well. Many artists, musicians, and writers find that channelling light language enhances their creativity and allows them to tap into a boundless source of inspiration. The spontaneous and intuitive nature of light language encourages free-flowing expression and experimentation, leading to the creation of art that resonates with deep spiritual significance. This creative process can be incredibly liberating, enabling individuals to express their innermost truths and emotions in a way that transcends conventional forms of communication.

Light language also plays a crucial role in community and collective healing. Group sessions and gatherings where light language is channeled can generate a powerful collective energy that amplifies the healing and transformational effects. These communal experiences foster a sense of unity and interconnectedness, creating a supportive environment where individuals can share their journeys and receive collective support. The resonance of light language in a group setting can elevate the vibrational frequency of the entire community, promoting collective harmony and well-being.

The applications and benefits of light language are vast and varied, encompassing personal healing, spiritual growth, energetic protection, communication with higher realms, creative expression, and collective healing. Its transformative power lies in its ability to connect with the deepest layers of the soul and the highest realms of consciousness, offering a direct and pure channel for divine energy and wisdom. As more individuals embrace and explore light language, its potential to transform and elevate human experience becomes increasingly evident, marking it as a profound and invaluable tool in spiritual evolution.

How Light Language Aids Healing

Introduction

Light Language, often referred to as the language of the soul, is a unique and powerful tool for spiritual and energetic healing. Unlike conventional languages, it transcends spoken words and operates on a vibrational level, communicating directly with the body, mind, and spirit. But how exactly does Light Language facilitate healing? This article explores the various ways in which Light Language aids in the healing process, helping individuals achieve emotional, mental, and physical well-being.

Vibrational Resonance and Healing

Light Language operates through vibrational resonance, meaning it works on the principle that everything in the universe, including our bodies, is made up of energy that vibrates at different frequencies. When someone speaks or channels Light Language, its unique frequencies resonate with the energy fields of individuals, initiating a process of alignment and balance.

1. Clearing Energy Blockages: One of the primary ways Light Language aids healing is by clearing blockages in the body's energy systems. These blockages, often caused by unresolved emotional trauma or negative thought patterns, can manifest as physical or emotional ailments. Light Language helps dissolve these blockages, allowing the free flow of energy and promoting healing.

2. Balancing Chakras: Chakras are the energy centres in the body that regulate various aspects of our physical, emotional, and spiritual well-being. Light Language can help balance and harmonise the chakras, ensuring that energy flows smoothly and efficiently throughout the body. This balance can lead to improved physical health, emotional stability, and heightened spiritual awareness.

Emotional and Mental Healing

Light Language also plays a significant role in emotional and mental healing. Its vibrational frequencies can penetrate deep into the subconscious mind, addressing and releasing unresolved emotions and thought patterns that may be causing distress.

1. Emotional Release: Many people carry emotional wounds from experiences that continue to affect their lives. Light Language helps facilitate the release of these suppressed emotions, bringing them to the surface to be acknowledged and healed. This process can lead to profound emotional relief and a greater sense of inner peace.

2. Mental Clarity: The energetic realignment brought about by Light Language can also clear mental fog and confusion. As Light Language removes blockages and allows energy to flow more freely, individuals often experience increased mental clarity, focus, and a greater sense of purpose.

Spiritual Awakening and Growth

Beyond physical and emotional healing, Light Language is a powerful catalyst for spiritual awakening and growth. It can help individuals connect with their higher selves and the divine, leading to profound spiritual insights and transformations.

1. Activation of Spiritual Gifts: Light Language can activate dormant spiritual gifts and abilities, such as heightened intuition, clairvoyance, and healing capabilities. This activation can help individuals realise their full potential and purpose in life.

2. Deepening Spiritual Connection: By attuning individuals to higher frequencies, Light Language facilitates a deeper connection with the divine and the universal consciousness. This connection can provide guidance, wisdom, and a profound sense of oneness with all that is.

DNA Activation and Cellular Healing

Recent explorations into Light Language suggest its potential for DNA activation and cellular healing. This concept revolves around the idea that Light Language can communicate with the body's cells and DNA, initiating profound changes at the molecular level.

1. People believe that Light Language awakens dormant aspects of our DNA, enhancing our physical, mental, and spiritual capacities in DNA Activation. This activation can lead to increased vitality, enhanced cognitive abilities, and a greater alignment with one's higher self.

2. Cellular Healing: On a cellular level, Light Language's vibrational frequencies can promote healing and regeneration. By communicating directly with the cells it can help repair damaged tissues, boost the immune system, and enhance overall physical health.

Light Language is a multifaceted tool for healing that operates on vibrational, emotional, mental, and spiritual levels. By clearing energy blockages, balancing chakras, facilitating emotional release, and promoting mental clarity, it aids in achieving holistic well-being.

Furthermore, its potential for DNA activation and cellular healing opens new avenues for profound physical and spiritual transformations. Whether you are seeking relief from physical ailments, emotional wounds, or a deeper spiritual connection, Light Language offers a unique and powerful pathway to healing and growth.

Chapter 6: Personal Stories and Experiences

Personal Stories and Experiences of Light Language

Awakening to Light Language: Jane's Healing Journey

Jane's Background

Jane had been struggling with chronic illness for years, feeling disconnected from her body and spirit. Traditional medical treatments offered limited relief, and she began exploring alternative healing modalities. Her journey led her to a holistic retreat where she was introduced to Light Language.

The First Encounter

During a guided meditation session at the retreat, Jane experienced her first encounter with Light Language. The facilitator began chanting in Light Language, and Jane felt an immediate resonance within her body. She described the experience as feeling vibrations throughout her cells, as if her body recognised the sounds on a deep, primal level.

Healing Process

Encouraged by this experience, Jane began incorporating Light Language into her daily routine. She would chant intuitively, allowing sounds to flow through her without overthinking. Over time, she noticed significant improvements in her health. Her chronic pain lessened, and she felt more energised and emotionally balanced. Jane attributed this transformation to the healing vibrations of Light Language, which seemed to align and harmonise her energy field.

Continuing the Journey

Jane continues to use Light Language as a part of her healing practice. She has learned to trust her intuitive guidance, allowing Light Language to emerge in different forms—whether through sounds, symbols, or movements. Her journey with Light Language has not only improved her physical health but also deepened her spiritual connection and understanding of herself.

Spiritual Awakening: Mark's Transformative Experience

Mark's Spiritual Quest

Mark had always been curious about spirituality, but never committed to any particular practice. His life felt monotonous, and he yearned for a deeper connection with the universe. His search for meaning led him to attend a spiritual retreat focusing on Light Language.

The Spontaneous Activation

During a group meditation, Mark experienced a spontaneous activation of Light Language. He suddenly felt a surge of energy and began speaking in a language he didn't consciously know. The words flowed effortlessly, accompanied by vivid imagery and a profound sense of peace. He later described this moment as feeling like a homecoming, as if he had reconnected with a lost part of himself.

Integrating Light Language

After the retreat, Mark dedicated himself to exploring Light Language further. He practiced daily, recording his sessions and reflecting on the symbols and messages that emerged. This practice brought about significant changes in his life. He developed a stronger sense of intuition, often receiving insights and guidance that proved beneficial in his personal and professional life.

Impact on Daily Life

Mark's use of Light Language has also enhanced his relationships. He feels more empathetic and connected to others, often using Light Language in his mind to send healing and positive intentions to those around him. The practice has become a cornerstone of his spiritual path, providing him with clarity, purpose, and a profound sense of interconnectedness.

Artistic Inspiration: Sofia's Creative Journey

Sofia's Artistic Background

Sofia is an abstract painter who always felt that her art was missing a deeper dimension. She experimented with various techniques and styles but struggled to convey the spiritual depth she sensed within herself. Her exploration led her to a workshop on Light Language for artists.

Discovering Light Language

The facilitator at the workshop introduced Sofia to the concept of using Light Language as a source of artistic inspiration. The facilitator encouraged participants to express themselves through spontaneous sounds and symbols, translating these into visual art. Sofia felt an immediate connection and began incorporating these elements into her work.

Transformative Art

The impact on Sofia's art was profound. She found that allowing Light Language to guide her creative process unlocked new levels of expression. Her paintings became more vibrant and dynamic, infused with a sense of movement and energy that resonated deeply with viewers. She received numerous comments about the transformative and healing qualities of her artwork.

Ongoing Exploration

Sofia continues to explore Light Language in her art. She uses it as a meditative practice, often beginning her painting sessions with chanting or drawing symbols intuitively. This approach has not only enhanced her creativity but also provided a deeper sense of fulfilment and connection to her spiritual path. Sofia's journey with Light Language has transformed her art and her understanding of creativity as a spiritual practice.

Testimonials from Light Language Practitioners

Emily's Testimonial

"Practicing Light Language has been a game-changer for me. It's like a direct line to my higher self. I use it in my daily meditation, and it has helped me navigate challenging emotions and situations with greater ease. The clarity and peace I feel after a session are unparalleled."

Michael's Testimonial

"Light Language has brought a new dimension to my energy healing practice. My clients report feeling a deep sense of relaxation and emotional release during sessions where I incorporate Light Language. It's as if the sounds and symbols bypass the conscious mind and work directly with the soul's energy."

Rachel's Testimonial

"Integrating Light Language into my yoga practice has been incredibly powerful. Chanting in Light Language during my sessions creates a sacred space and amplifies the healing energy. I feel more connected to my body and spirit, and my students have shared similar experiences of heightened awareness and spiritual connection."

In Summary

The personal stories and testimonials shared here highlight the transformative power of Light Language. Whether used for healing, spiritual awakening, or creative expression, Light Language resonates on a deep, intuitive level, unlocking new dimensions of experience and understanding. These experiences serve as a testament to the profound impact Light Language can have on our lives, offering a path to greater clarity, connection, and spiritual growth.

Chapter 7 The Future of Light Language: A Path to Global Transformation

Light Language, a multidimensional form of communication involving sounds, symbols, and movements, has been gaining traction in recent years as people seek deeper spiritual connections and alternative methods of healing. Rooted in ancient traditions yet evolving with modern insights, Light Language offers a promising avenue for personal and collective transformation. As we look to the future, its potential to impact various aspects of society becomes increasingly apparent.

The Growing Popularity of Light Language

Spiritual Awakening and Personal Growth

In an age where spiritual awakening is becoming more common, Light Language serves as a powerful tool for individuals seeking to deepen their connection with the universe. Many people report profound experiences of healing, increased intuition, and heightened states of consciousness when practicing Light Language. As more individuals share their stories and experiences, the collective understanding and acceptance of this ancient practice grow, paving the way for its integration into mainstream spiritual practices.

Healing and Wellness

Light Language has shown significant promise in the realm of holistic healing. Practitioners use it to balance energy fields, release emotional blockages, and promote physical well-being. Many believe that the vibrational frequencies of Light Language resonate with the body's energy centres, facilitating deep healing. As scientific interest in alternative medicine continues to expand, Light Language could become a recognised modality within the broader field of energy healing.

Scientific Exploration and Validation

Neuroplasticity and Cognitive Benefits

Emerging research into neuroplasticity—the brain's ability to reorganise itself by forming new neural connections—suggests that engaging in novel activities like Light Language can stimulate cognitive growth and flexibility. Future studies may explore how Light Language affects brain function, emotional regulation, and overall mental health. Such scientific validation could bolster its credibility and encourage broader acceptance.

Frequency and Vibration Research

The scientific community is increasingly interested in the effects of sound and vibration on human health. Research into the frequencies used in Light Language could uncover insights into how these sounds impact cellular function, emotional well-being, and spiritual experiences. Understanding these mechanisms could lead to the development of new therapeutic techniques and technologies.

Integration into Modern Life

Education and Personal Development

As Light Language becomes more widely recognised, its applications in education and personal development are likely to expand. Workshops, courses, and online platforms dedicated to teaching Light Language can help individuals develop their intuitive and creative abilities. Integrating Light Language practices into educational curricula could also foster emotional intelligence and spiritual awareness in students.

Technology and Innovation

Advancements in technology could revolutionise the practice and dissemination of Light Language. Virtual reality (VR) and augmented reality (AR) experiences could provide immersive environments for learning and practicing Light Language, enhancing the user experience. Additionally, apps and digital tools designed to analyse and interpret Light Language symbols and sounds could make the practice more accessible to a broader audience.

Community and Global Impact

Collective Consciousness

As more people engage with Light Language, the collective consciousness could experience a shift towards greater harmony and interconnectedness. This shift could facilitate global efforts towards peace, environmental stewardship, and social justice. Light Language has the potential to unify diverse communities through a shared spiritual practice that transcends linguistic and cultural barriers.

Cultural Preservation and Innovation

Light Language can also play a role in preserving ancient wisdom and cultural heritage. By reviving and modernising ancient practices, we honour our ancestors while adapting their wisdom to contemporary contexts. This balance of preservation and innovation ensures that Light Language remains relevant and impactful for future generations.

Challenges and Considerations

Skepticism and Misunderstanding

Despite its growing popularity, Light Language may still face skepticism and misunderstanding. It is essential for practitioners and advocates to communicate its benefits clearly and respectfully, bridging the gap between ancient traditions and modern science. Collaborative efforts between spiritual communities and scientific researchers can help validate and demystify Light Language.

Ethical Practice

As Light Language gains traction, maintaining ethical standards in its practice and teaching becomes crucial. Ensuring that practitioners are well-trained and respectful of the cultural origins of Light Language will help preserve its integrity and authenticity. Transparency, inclusivity, and respect for diverse spiritual paths will foster a healthy and supportive community.

Summary

The future of Light Language is bright with possibilities. Its potential to enhance personal growth, holistic healing, and collective consciousness positions it as a transformative force in the 21st century. As we embrace this ancient practice with modern insights, Light Language can guide us towards a more harmonious, connected, and enlightened world. By bridging the gap between ancient wisdom and contemporary science, we unlock new dimensions of human potential and pave the way for a future where Light Language is an integral part of our spiritual and everyday lives.

Chapter 8 Ethical Considerations

Light language, as a multidimensional form of communication and healing, brings with it several ethical considerations when integrated into holistic practices. These considerations are crucial for ensuring that the use of light language is respectful, responsible, and beneficial for all involved. Here are the key ethical considerations for practitioners and recipients of light language:

Informed Consent

Clear Communication: Practitioners must clearly explain what light language is, how it works, and what clients can expect during a session. This ensures that clients have a thorough understanding before consenting to the practice.

Voluntary Participation: Clients should participate willingly and without any pressure. Informed consent involves ensuring that clients know they can opt -out at any time.

Cultural Sensitivity and Respect

Respect for Traditions: Light language often incorporates elements that may be similar to practices in indigenous and other traditional cultures. Practitioners must approach these elements with respect and avoid cultural appropriation.

Acknowledging Sources: When using techniques or knowledge derived from specific cultures, it's important to acknowledge these sources and show gratitude for the wisdom shared.

Professional Boundaries

Scope of Practice: Practitioners should work within the boundaries of their training and expertise. They should not claim to provide medical or psychological diagnosis unless they are licensed professionals in those fields.

Referral to Specialists: If a client's needs are beyond the practitioner's scope, they should refer the client to an appropriate specialist, such as a licensed therapist, doctor, or other qualified professional.

Confidentiality

Privacy Protection: Clients' personal information and the content of their sessions should be kept confidential. Practitioners must have clear policies on how client information is stored and shared.

Anonymity: When discussing case studies or experiences publicly or in educational settings, practitioners should anonymise details to protect client identities.

Authenticity and Integrity

Genuine Practice: Practitioners should ensure that their use of light language is genuine and not performed for show or financial gain. Authenticity in practice builds trust and maintains the integrity of the work.

Truthfulness: Be honest about the practitioner's qualifications, experience, and the potential benefits and limitations of light language.

Non-Harm and Beneficence

Healing Intention: The primary intention should always be to benefit the client. Practitioners should avoid any practices that could cause harm or distress.

Energy Management: Practitioners should be well-versed in energy management to ensure they do not unintentionally transmit negative energies to clients.

Client Empowerment

Encouraging Self-Agency: Practitioners should encourage clients to trust their own intuition and inner guidance. The goal is to empower clients rather than create dependency on the practitioner.

Providing Tools: Offer clients tools and techniques they can use independently to continue their healing and spiritual growth outside of sessions.

Ongoing Education and Self-Reflection

Continual Learning: Practitioners should commit to ongoing education and personal development to stay updated with new insights and methods in holistic practices.

Self-Reflection and Accountability: Regular self-reflection and peer reviews can help practitioners stay aligned with ethical standards and improve their practice.

Transparency and Honesty

Transparent Pricing: Be clear and upfront about the cost of services. Avoid hidden fees or upselling additional services in a way that could be considered exploitative.

Honest Marketing: Marketing materials should accurately represent the services provided and not make exaggerated claims about outcomes.

Respecting Individual Beliefs

Non-Dogmatic Approach: Practitioners should respect the diverse spiritual and personal beliefs of their clients. Practitioners should offer light language as a tool for those who resonate with it, without imposing beliefs.

Flexibility and Adaptability: Be willing to adapt practices to better align with the client's belief system and comfort level.

Summary

Integrating light language into holistic practices requires careful consideration of ethical principles to ensure it is used responsibly and respectfully. Practitioners must prioritise informed consent, cultural sensitivity, professional boundaries, confidentiality, authenticity, non-harm, client empowerment, ongoing education, transparency, and respect for individual beliefs. By adhering to these ethical considerations, practitioners can create a safe, respectful, and effective environment for their clients, facilitating genuine healing and spiritual growth.

Chapter 9 Light Language And The Law Of Manifestation

Light language and the law of manifestation are powerful tools that, when combined, can significantly enhance your ability to create and attract your desired reality. Here's how to implement light language in the context of the law of manifestation:

Understanding Light Language and the Law of Manifestation

Light Language: A multidimensional form of communication that transcends traditional spoken language. It consists of sounds, symbols, movements, and frequencies that can heal, activate, and transform on a deep energetic level.

Law of Manifestation: A principle stating that thoughts, beliefs, and emotions can shape reality. By focusing on positive intentions and aligning with the desired outcome, you can manifest your goals and dreams.

In the journey of manifestation, the universe often works in mysterious and unexpected ways. Although we have clear intentions and visualise specific outcomes, the path to achieving our desires can be unpredictable. Remaining receptive to opportunities and signals from the universe is vital for acknowledging and embracing serendipitous moments.

Steps to Implement Light Language in Manifestation

Set a Clear Intention

Define Your Desire: Be specific about what you want to manifest. Clarity helps direct the energy more effectively.

Visualise the Outcome: Create a vivid mental picture of your desired reality. Feel the emotions associated with achieving this goal.

Create a Sacred Space

Environment: Choose a quiet, comfortable place where you won't be disturbed. This can be a meditation room, a corner of your home, or a spot in nature.

Cleanse the Space: Use sage, palo santo, or sound (like a bell or singing bowl) to clear any negative energy.

Connect with Light Language

Meditation: Begin with a meditation to centre yourself and connect with your higher self or spiritual guides.

Channel Light Language: Allow light language to flow through you. This could be through speaking, singing, toning, hand gestures, or drawing symbols. Trust the process and let it be spontaneous.

Infuse Your Intention with Light Language

Speak or Sing Your Intention: Use light language to vocalise your intention. Imagine the sounds and frequencies carrying your desire out into the universe.

Draw Symbols: If you receive symbols during your light language session, draw them out and place them somewhere you can see them daily.

Use Movement: Incorporate body movements or gestures that feel aligned with your intention. This helps to anchor the energy in your physical body and the material world.

Amplify with Emotion

Feel the Emotions: Emotions are powerful amplifiers of energy. Feel the joy, gratitude, and excitement of already having manifested your desire.

Gratitude: Express deep gratitude for the manifestation as if it has already occurred. Gratitude raises your vibration and aligns you with the energy of receiving.

Release and Trust

Let Go: Once you've infused your intention with light language and emotion, release it into the universe. Trust that the energy will work in your favour.

Detach from Outcome: Detach from the need to control how and when the manifestation will occur. Trust in the divine timing and the wisdom of the universe.

Take Inspired Action

Act on Intuition: Pay attention to any intuitive nudges or inspirations that come your way. Taking inspired action aligns your physical reality with your energetic intentions.

Be Open: Stay open to opportunities and signs from the universe. Sometimes manifestations come in unexpected ways. Staying open to opportunities and signs from the universe is a crucial aspect of successful manifestation.

It requires a flexible mindset, trust in the universe's wisdom, and heightened awareness of subtle cues. By embracing the unexpected and acting on intuitive guidance, we align ourselves more closely with the flow of universal energy, allowing our desires to manifest in ways that are often more profound and fulfilling than we initially imagined. This openness transforms the journey of manifestation into a dynamic, co-creative dance with the universe, filled with wonder, growth, and endless possibilities.

Regular Practice

Consistency: Regularly practise light language and manifestation techniques. Consistency helps to build and maintain the energetic momentum.

Reflection: Periodically reflect on your progress, adjust your intentions if necessary, and continue to align with your highest good.

Tips for Enhancing the Practice

Journal: Keep a journal to document your intentions, light language sessions, and any signs or manifestations that occur. This helps track progress and refine your practice.

Community: Join a community of like-minded individuals who practise light language and manifestation. Sharing experiences and techniques can enhance your understanding and effectiveness.

Self-Care: Maintain a healthy body and mind through proper nutrition, exercise, and rest. A well-balanced body supports higher energetic work.

Summary

Combining light language with the law of manifestation is a powerful practice that aligns your energetic frequency with your desired outcomes. By setting clear intentions, creating a sacred space, connecting with light language, and infusing your desires with emotion and trust, you can effectively manifest your goals and dreams. Regular practice, self-reflection, and taking inspired action are key to maintaining momentum and achieving success. Embrace the process with an open heart and mind, and watch as your reality transforms in alignment with your highest intentions.

Chapter 10 The Power of Internal Channelling in Light Language: Unlocking Deeper Rewards

In the realm of spiritual practices, light language stands out as a profound tool for personal transformation, healing, and connection with higher realms. The manner in which one channels light language — whether internally or externally — can significantly influence the outcomes and rewards of this practice. While external channelling, which involves seeking guidance from outside sources such as other practitioners or spiritual entities, has its merits, internal channelling, which focuses on tapping into one's own inner wisdom and intuitive faculties, often brings deeper and more sustainable rewards. This chapter explores the reasons why internal dialogue can be more beneficial and how it enhances the practice of light language.

Internal channelling fosters a direct and personal connection with the source of light language. By turning inward, practitioners tap into their own higher self, soul, and innate wisdom. This connection is unmediated and pure, allowing for a more authentic and individualised experience. It ensures that the messages and energies received are perfectly aligned with the practitioner's unique path and needs. When light language is channelled internally, it resonates deeply within the individual, creating a profound sense of alignment and coherence that external sources may not always provide.

A key advantage of internal channelling is the empowerment it offers. Relying on external sources for spiritual guidance can sometimes create dependency, diminishing one's confidence in their own intuitive abilities. Internal channelling, on the other hand, cultivates self-reliance and trust in one's inner voice. This empowerment extends beyond the practice of light language, permeating all areas of life. As individuals learn to trust their inner guidance, they become more confident in their decisions and actions, leading to a greater sense of autonomy and personal sovereignty.

Furthermore, internal channelling allows for a deeper level of self-discovery and healing. When practitioners engage in light language through their own inner channels, they are often guided to address and heal their subconscious blocks, traumas, and limiting beliefs. This self-directed healing process can be more effective and transformative than receiving generalised guidance from external sources. Internal channelling facilitates a tailored approach to healing, where the practitioner is intuitively led to the specific areas that need attention, resulting in more profound and lasting change.

The practice of internal channelling also enhances the development of intuitive and psychic abilities. Regularly tuning into one's inner guidance and channelling light language internally strengthens the neural pathways associated with intuition and higher perception. Over time, practitioners become more adept at receiving and interpreting subtle energies and messages. This heightened intuition can be a valuable asset in all aspects of life, enabling individuals to navigate challenges with greater clarity and insight.

Another significant benefit of internal channelling is the deepened sense of connection it fosters with the divine and the higher self. By turning inward, practitioners create a sacred space within themselves where they can commune with higher realms and their true essence. This inner sanctuary becomes a source of comfort, inspiration, and spiritual nourishment. The connection established through internal channeling is often more intimate and enduring than the fleeting connections experienced through external sources.

Internal channeling also encourages a more grounded and integrated approach to spirituality. When practitioners rely on their inner guidance, they are more likely to remain grounded and present in their physical reality.

This integration of spiritual and material aspects of life is crucial for holistic well-being. It ensures that spiritual insights and energies are effectively embodied and manifested in the physical world, rather than remaining abstract or disconnected.

In conclusion, internal channeling offers numerous advantages over external channeling in the practice of light language. It fosters a direct and personal connection with the source, empowers individuals, facilitates deep self-discovery and healing, enhances intuitive abilities, deepens spiritual connection, and promotes a grounded and integrated approach to spirituality. By turning inward and trusting their inner wisdom, practitioners can unlock deeper and more sustainable rewards, leading to a more fulfilling and transformative spiritual journey.

Chapter 11 The Role of Light Language in Assisting A Spirits Transition

Spirits Light language, a multifaceted spiritual practice, transcends conventional linguistic boundaries and communicates directly with the soul through sound, symbols, and movement. Its capacity to facilitate healing, transformation, and spiritual connection has been widely recognised. One profound application of light language is its potential to assist spirits in transitioning to the afterlife. This essay explores how light language can help spirits move on, delving into its energetic properties, communicative abilities, and the compassionate intention behind its practice.

The process of assisting spirits in their transition to the afterlife involves addressing the energetic and emotional residues that may bind them to the earthly plane. Light language, with its high-frequency vibrations, can effectively cleanse and purify these residual energies. The sounds and symbols inherent in light language resonate at a level that transcends the physical, reaching into the spiritual realms where these energies reside. By channelling light language, practitioners can create a vibrational environment that encourages the release of attachments, fears, and unresolved emotions that may be holding a spirit back.

Communication is another crucial aspect of assisting spirits in their journey to the afterlife. Spirits often remain attached to the earthly plane due to unfinished business, unspoken words, or the need for closure. Light language, as a universal form of communication, bypasses the limitations of human languages and directly conveys messages of love, forgiveness, and peace. This form of communication can be profoundly healing for spirits, providing them with the assurance and understanding needed to move forward. The practitioner acts as a compassionate intermediary, channelling these messages through light language to help the spirit find resolution and peace.

The compassionate intention behind light language plays a significant role in assisting spirits. Practitioners who engage in this work do so with a deep sense of empathy and a genuine desire to aid the spirit in its transition. This compassionate energy is infused into the light language, further amplifying its effectiveness. The spirit can sense the loving and supportive intention behind the practice, which can provide the comfort and encouragement needed to let go of earthly ties and move towards the light.

Light language can open and activate energetic pathways, both within the practitioner and the spirit. These pathways, often referred to as meridians or energy channels, can become blocked or stagnant, hindering the spirit's progress. By channelling light language, the practitioner can help to clear and activate these pathways, facilitating a smoother and more natural transition. The activation of these pathways can also enhance the spirit's connection to higher realms, making the journey to the afterlife less daunting and more inviting.

Furthermore, the use of light language in rituals and ceremonies dedicated to honouring and releasing spirits can be highly effective. These rituals often incorporate elements such as sound, movement, and sacred symbols, all of which are integral to light language. The ceremonial aspect provides a structured and respectful environment in which the spirit can be acknowledged and released. Using light language in these settings can elevate the ritual, creating a powerful energetic space that supports the spirit's transition.

The practitioner's role in this process is to offer guidance and support. By maintaining a high vibrational state and a clear intention, the practitioner becomes a beacon of light for the spirit, illuminating the path to the afterlife. The practitioner's connection to higher realms strengthened through the practice of light language, serves as a bridge between the earthly and spiritual planes. This bridge provides the spirit with a clear and safe passage, reducing any fear or hesitation associated with moving on.

In conclusion, light language offers a unique and powerful means of assisting spirits in their transition to the afterlife. Through its high-frequency vibrations, universal communication, compassionate intention, and ability to clear and activate energetic pathways, light language provides the necessary support for spirits to release their earthly ties and move towards the light.

Practitioners who engage in this sacred work do so with a deep sense of empathy and a commitment to facilitating the spirit's journey. By creating a loving and supportive environment, they help to ensure that the spirit's transition is peaceful and harmonious. In this way, light language serves as a bridge to the afterlife, guiding spirits towards their next phase of existence with grace and compassion.

Chapter 12 Conclusion: Embracing Light Language

As we journey through the mystical and transformative world of Light Language, we uncover an ancient yet ever-evolving form of communication that transcends conventional speech. Light Language is more than just sounds and symbols; it is a bridge connecting us to the cosmos, our higher selves, and the collective consciousness of humanity. This profound practice, rooted in ancient traditions and revitalised in modern contexts, offers limitless possibilities for personal and global transformation.

The Power of Light Language

Light Language empowers us to heal on multiple levels—physically, emotionally, mentally, and spiritually. It taps into the vibrational frequencies of the universe, realigning our energies and awakening dormant potentials within our DNA. Through the science of neuroplasticity, we understand how Light Language can rewire our brains, enhancing cognitive flexibility and emotional resilience. This practice fosters creativity, intuition, and a deep sense of connection to the world around us.

A Tool for Modern Times

In today's fast-paced and often fragmented world, Light Language serves as a beacon of harmony and integration. It offers a unique blend of ancient wisdom and contemporary relevance, providing tools for healing, spiritual growth, and creative expression. As more people embrace Light Language, we witness the formation of a global community united by a shared quest for higher consciousness and deeper understanding.

Integrating Light Language into Our Lives

The stories and experiences shared in this book highlight the transformative potential of Light Language. Whether through personal healing, artistic inspiration, or spiritual awakening, Light Language touches the core of our being, inviting us to explore new dimensions of existence. By integrating Light Language into our daily practices— through meditation, creative expression, or holistic healing—we unlock its full potential and invite profound shifts in our lives.

A Path to Collective Evolution

The rise of Light Language signals a broader shift towards collective evolution. As individuals awaken to their true potential, they contribute to a larger movement of global awakening and unity. Light Language can help us navigate the challenges of our times, fostering empathy, compassion, and a deeper sense of interconnectedness. It reminds us that we are all part of a greater tapestry of existence, woven together by the universal language of light and love.

Embracing the Future with Light Language

As we look to the future, the possibilities for Light Language are limitless. Its integration into education, technology, and community practices will continue to expand, offering new avenues for exploration and growth. By embracing Light Language, we open ourselves to a world of infinite potential, where healing, creativity, and spiritual connection are within everyone's reach.

Final Thoughts

The journey with Light Language is deeply personal yet universally resonant. It is a reminder of our innate ability to connect with the divine and with each other in profound and meaningful ways. As you continue to explore and practice Light Language, may you find healing, inspiration, and a deeper sense of purpose. Let Light Language be a guiding light on your path, illuminating the way to a brighter, more harmonious future.

Embrace the light, speak the language, and let the transformation begin.

"Light therapy is not just a treatment; it's an awakening of the soul, a gentle reminder that within us all lies an innate capacity for healing, guided by the radiant energy of the universe."

Paula Wratten